THE GREEN BOOK: BY MUAMMAR GADDAFI

TABLE OF CONTENTS

TABLE OF CONTENTS

TABLE OF CONTENTS

PART 2: THE SOLUTION OF THE ECONOMIC PROBLEM: SOCIALISM: 56-94

TABLE OF CONTENTS

PART 1: THE SOLUTION OF THE PROBLEM OF DEMOCRACY: THE AUTHORITY OF THE PEOPLE

1. THE INSTRUMENT OF GOVERNMENT

The instrument of government is the prime political problem confronting human communities (The problem of the instrument of government entails questions of the following kind. What form should the exercise of authority assume? How ought societies to organize themselves politically in the modern world?)

Even conflict within the family is often the result of the failure to resolve this problem of authority. It has clearly become more serious with the emergence of modern societies.

People today face this persistent question in new and pressing ways. Communities are exposed to the risks of uncertainty, and suffer the grave consequences of wrong answers. Yet none has succeeded in answering it conclusively and democratically. THE GREEN BOOK presents the ultimate solution to the problem of the proper instrument of government.

All political systems in the world today are a product of the struggle for power between alternative instruments of government. This struggle may be peaceful or armed, as is evidenced among classes, sects, tribes, parties or individuals. The outcome is always the victory of a particular governing structure - be it that of an individual, group, party or class - and the defeat of the people; the defeat of genuine democracy.

Political struggle that results in the victory of a candidate with, for example, 51 per cent of the votes leads to a dictatorial governing body in the guise of a false democracy, since 49 per cent of the electorate is ruled by an instrument of government they did not vote for, but which has been imposed upon them. Such is dictatorship. Besides, this political conflict may produce a governing body that represents only a minority. For when votes are distributed among several candidates, though one polls more than any other, the sum of the votes received by those who received fewer votes might well constitute an overwhelming majority. However, the candidate with fewer votes wins and his success is regarded as legitimate and democratic! In actual fact, dictatorship is established under the cover of false democracy. This is the reality of the political systems prevailing in the world today. They are dictatorial systems and it is evident that they falsify genuine democracy.

2. PARLIAMENTS

Parliaments are the backbone of that conventional democracy prevailing in the world today. Parliament is a misrepresentation of the people, and parliamentary systems are a false solution to the problem of democracy. A parliament is originally founded to represent the people, but this in itself is undemocratic as democracy means the authority of the people and not an authority acting on their behalf. The mere existence of a parliament means the absence of the people. True democracy exists only through the direct participation of the people, and not through the activity of their representatives. Parliaments have been a legal barrier between the people and the exercise of authority, excluding the masses from meaningful politics and monopolizing sovereignty in their place. People are left with only a facade of democracy, manifested in long queues to cast their election ballots.

To lay bare the character of parliaments, one has to examine their origin. They are either elected from constituencies, a party, or a coalition of parties, or are appointed. But all of these procedures are undemocratic, for dividing the population into constituencies means that one member of parliament represents thousands, hundreds of thousands, or millions of people, depending on the size of the population. It also means that a member keeps few popular organizational links with the electors since he, like other members, is considered a representative of the whole people. This is what the prevailing traditional democracy requires. The masses are completely isolated from the representative and he, in turn, is totally removed from them. Immediately after winning the electors' votes the representative takes over the people's sovereignty and acts on their behalf. The prevailing traditional democracy endows the member of parliament with a sacredness and immunity which are denied to the rest of the people. Parliaments, therefore, have become a means of plundering and usurping the authority of the people. It has thus become the right of the people to struggle, through popular revolution, to destroy such instruments - the so-called parliamentary assemblies which usurp democracy and sovereignty, and which stifle the will of the people. The masses have the right to proclaim reverberantly the new principle: no representation in lieu of the people.

If parliament is formed from one party as a result of its winning an election, it becomes a parliament of the winning party and not of the people. It represents the party and not the people, and the executive power of the parliament becomes that of the victorious party and not of the people. The same is true of the parliament of proportional representation in which each party holds a number of seats proportional to their success in the popular vote. The members of the parliament represent their respective parties and not the people, and the power established by such a coalition is the power of the combined parties and not that of the people. Under such systems, the people are the victims whose votes are vied for by exploitative competing factions who dupe the people into political circuses that are outwardly noisy and frantic, but inwardly powerless and irrelevant. Alternatively, the people are seduced into standing in long, apathetic, silent queues to cast their ballots in the same way that they throw waste paper into dustbins. This is the traditional democracy prevalent in the whole world, whether it is represented by a one-party, two-party, multiparty or non-party system. Thus it is clear that representation is a fraud.

Moreover, since the system of elected parliaments is based on propaganda to win votes, it is a demagogic system in the real sense of the word. Votes can be bought and falsified. Poor people are unable to compete in the election campaigns, and the result is that only the rich get elected. Assemblies constituted by appointment or hereditary succession do not fall under any form of democracy.

Philosophers, thinkers, and writers advocated the theory of representative parliaments at a time when peoples were unconsciously herded like sheep by kings, sultans and conquerors. The ultimate aspiration of the people of those times was to have someone to represent them before such rulers. When even this aspiration was rejected, people waged bitter and protracted struggle to attain this goal.

After the successful establishment of the age of the republics and the beginning of the era of the masses, it is unthinkable that democracy should mean the electing of only a few representatives to act on behalf of great masses. This is an obsolete structure. Authority must be in the hands of all of the people.

The most tyrannical dictatorships the world has known have existed under the aegis of parliaments.

3. THE PARTY

The party is a contemporary form of dictatorship. It is the modern instrument of dictatorial government. The party is the rule of a part over the whole. As a party is not an individual, it creates a superficial democracy by establishing assemblies, committees, and propaganda through its members. The party is not a democratic instrument because it is composed only of those people who have common interests, a common perception or a shared culture; or those who belong to the same region or share the same belief. They form a party to achieve their ends, impose their will, or extend the dominion of their beliefs, values, and interests to the society as a whole. A party's aim is to achieve power under the pretext of carrying out its program. Democratically, none of these parties should govern a whole people who constitute a diversity of interests, ideas, temperaments, regions and beliefs. The party is a dictatorial instrument of government that enables those with common outlooks or interests to rule the people as a whole. Within the community, the party represents a minority.

The purpose of forming a party is to create an instrument to rule the people, i.e., to rule over non-members of the party. The party is, fundamentally, based on an arbitrary authoritarian concept - the domination of the members of the party over the rest of the people. The party presupposes that its accession to power is the way to attain its ends, and assumes that its objectives are also those of the people. This is the theory justifying party dictatorship, and is the basis of any dictatorship. No matter how many parties exist, the theory remains valid.

The existence of many parties intensifies the struggle for power, and this results in the neglect of any achievements for the people and of any socially beneficial plans. Such actions are presented as a justification to undermine the position of the ruling party so that an opposing party can replace it. The parties very seldom resort to arms in their struggle but, rather, denounce and denigrate the actions of each other. This is a battle which is inevitably waged at the expense of the higher, vital interests of the society. Some, if not all, of those higher interests will fall prey to the struggle for power between instruments of government, for the destruction of those interests supports the opposition in their argument against the ruling party or parties. In order to rule, the opposition party has to defeat the existing instrument of government.

To do so, the opposition must minimize the government's achievements and cast doubt on its plans, even though those plans may be beneficial to the society. Consequently, the interests and programs of the society become the victims of the parties' struggle for power. Such struggle is, therefore, politically, socially, and economically destructive to the society, despite the fact that it creates political activity.

Thus, the struggle results in the victory of another instrument of government; the fall of one party, and the rise of another. It is, in fact, a defeat for the people, i.e., a defeat for democracy. Furthermore, parties can be bribed and corrupted either from inside or outside.

Originally, the party is formed ostensibly to represent the people. Subsequently, the party leadership becomes representative of the membership, and the leader represents the party elite. It becomes clear that this partisan game is a deceitful farce based on a false form of democracy. It has a selfish authoritarian character based on maneuvres, intrigues and political games. This confirms the fact that the party system is a modern instrument of dictatorship. The party system is an outright, unconvincing dictatorship, one which the world has not yet surpassed. It is, in fact, the dictatorship of the modern age.

The parliament of the winning party is indeed a parliament of the party, for the executive power formed by this parliament is the power of the party over the people. Party power, which is supposedly for the good of the whole people, is actually the arch-enemy of a fraction of the people, namely, the opposition party or parties and their supporters. The opposition is, therefore, not a popular check on the ruling party but, rather, is itself opportunistically seeking to replace the ruling party. According to modern democracy, the legitimate check on the ruling party is the parliament, the majority of whose members are from that ruling party. That is to say, control is in the hands of the ruling party, and power is in the hands of the controlling party. Thus the deception, falseness and invalidity of the political theories dominant in the world today become obvious. From these emerge contemporary conventional democracy.

"The party represents a segment of the people, but the sovereignty of the people is indivisible."

"The party allegedly governs on behalf of the people, but in reality the true principle of democracy is based upon the notion that there can be no representation in lieu of the people."

The party system is the modern equivalent of the tribal or sectarian system. A society governed by one party is similar to one which is governed by one tribe or one sect. The party, as shown, represents the perception of a certain group of people, or the interests of one group in society, or one belief, or one region. Such a party is a minority compared with the whole people, just as the tribe and the sect are. The minority has narrow, common sectarian interests and beliefs, from which a common outlook is formed. Only the blood-relationship distinguishes a tribe from a party, and, indeed, a tribe might also be the basis for the foundation of a party. There is no difference between party struggle and tribal or sectarian struggles for power. Just as tribal and sectarian rule is politically unacceptable and inappropriate, likewise the rule under a party system. Both follow the same path and lead to the same end. The negative and destructive effects of the tribal or sectarian struggle on society is identical to the negative and destructive effects of the party struggle.

4. CLASS

The political class system is the same as a party, tribal, or sectarian system since a class dominates society in the same way that a party, tribe or sect would. Classes, like parties, sects or tribes, are groups of people within society who share common interests. Common interests arise from the existence of a group of people bound together by blood-relationship, belief, culture, locality or standard of living. Classes, parties, sects and tribes emerge because blood-relationship, social rank, economic interest, standard of living, belief, culture and locality create a common outlook to achieve a common end. Thus, social structures, in the form of classes, parties, tribes or sects, emerge. These eventually develop into political entities directed toward the realization of the goals of that group. In all cases, the people are neither the class, the party, the tribe, nor the sect, for these are no more than a segment of the people and constitute a minority. If a class, a party, a tribe, or a sect dominates a society, then the dominant system becomes a dictatorship. However, a class or a tribal coalition is preferable to a party coalition since societies originally consisted of tribal communities. One seldom finds a group of people who do not belong to a tribe, and all people belong to a specific class. But no party or parties embrace all of the people, and therefore the party or party coalition represents a minority compared to the masses outside their membership. Under genuine democracy, there can be no justification for any one class to subdue other classes for its interests. Similarly, no party, tribe or sect can crush others for their own interests.

To allow such actions abandons the logic of democracy and justifies resort to the use of force. Such policies of suppression are dictatorial because they are not in the interest of the whole society, which consists of more than one class, tribe or sect, or the members of one party. There is no justification for such actions, though the dictatorial argument is that society actually consists of numerous segments, one of which must undertake the liquidation of others in order to remain solely in power. This exercise is not, accordingly, in the interests of the whole society but, rather, in the interests of a specific class, tribe, sect, party, or those who claim to speak for the society. Such an act is basically aimed at the member of the society who does not belong to the party, class, tribe or sect which carries out the liquidation.

A society torn apart by party feud is similar to one which is torn apart by tribal or sectarian conflicts.

A party that is formed in the name of a class inevitably becomes a substitute for that class and continues in the process of spontaneous transformation until it becomes hostile to the class that it replaces.

Any class which inherits a society also inherits its characteristics. If the working class, for example, subdues all other classes of a particular society, it then becomes its only heir and forms its material and social base. The heir acquires the traits of those from whom it inherits, though this may not be evident all at once. With the passage of time, characteristics of the other eliminated classes will emerge within the ranks of the working class itself. The members of the new society will assume the attitudes and perspectives appropriate to their newly evolved characteristics. Thus, the working class will develop a separate society possessing all of the contradictions of the old society. In the first stage, the material standard and importance of the members become unequal. Thereafter, groups emerge which automatically become classes that are the same as the classes that were eliminated. Thus, the struggle for domination of the society begins again. Each group of people, each faction, and each new class will all vie to become the instrument of government.

Being social in nature, the material base of any society is changeable. The instrument of government of this material base may be sustained for some time, but it will eventual become obsolete as new material and social standards evolve to form a new material base. Any society which undergoes a class conflict may at one time have been a one-class society but, through evolution, inevitably becomes a multi-class society.

The class that expropriates and acquires the possession of others to maintain power for itself will soon find that, through evolution, it will be itself subject to change as though it were the society as a whole.

In summary, all attempts at unifying the material base of a society in order to solve the problem of government, or at putting an end to the struggle in favour of a party, class, sect or tribe have failed. All endeavours aimed at appeasing the masses through the election of representatives or through parliaments have equally failed. To continue such practices would be a waste of time and a mockery of the people.

5. PLEBISCITES

Plebiscites are a fraud against democracy. Those who vote "yes" or "no" do not, in fact, express their free will but, rather, are silenced by the modern conception of democracy as they are not allowed to say more than "yes" or "no". Such a system is oppressive and tyrannical. Those who vote "no" should express their reasons and why they did not say "yes", and those who say "yes" should verify such agreement and why they did not vote "no". Both should state their wishes and be able to justify their "yes" or "no" vote.

What then, is the path to be taken by humanity in order to conclusively rid itself of the elements of dictatorship and tyranny?

The intricate problem in the case of democracy is reflected in the nature of the instrument of government, which is demonstrated by conflicts of classes, parties and individuals. The elections and plebiscites were invented to cover the failure of these unsuccessful experiments to solve this problem. The solution lies in finding an instrument of government other than those which are subject to conflict and which represent only one faction of society; that is to say, an instrument of government which is not a party class, sect or a tribe, but an instrument of government which is the people as a whole. In other words, we seek an instrument of government which neither represents the people nor speaks in their name.

There can be no representation in lieu of the people and representation is fraud. If such an instrument can be found, then the problem is solved and true popular democracy is realized. Thus, humankind would have terminated the eras of tyranny and dictatorships, and replaced them with the authority of the people.

THE GREEN BOOK presents the ultimate solution to the problem of the instrument of government, and indicates for the masses the path upon which they can advance from the age of dictatorship to that of genuine democracy.

This new theory is based on the authority of the people, without representation or deputation. It achieves direct democracy in an orderly and effective form. It is superior to the older attempts at direct democracy which were impractical because they lacked popular organizations at base levels.

6. POPULAR CONFERENCES AND PEOPLE'S COMMITTEES

Popular Conferences are the only means to achieve popular democracy. Any system of government contrary to this method, the method of Popular Conferences, is undemocratic. All the prevailing systems of government in the world today will remain undemocratic, unless they adopt this method. Popular Conferences are the end of the journey of the masses in quest of democracy.

Popular Conferences and People's Committees are the fruition of the people's struggle for democracy. Popular Conferences and People's Committees are not creations of the imagination; they are the product of thought which has absorbed all human experiments to achieve democracy.

Direct democracy, if put into practice, is indisputably the ideal method of government.

Because it is impossible to gather all people, however small the population, in one place so that they can discuss, discern and decide policies, nations departed from direct democracy, which became an utopian idea detached from reality. It was replaced by various theories of government, such as representative councils, party-coalitions and plebiscites, all of which isolated the masses and prevented them from managing their political affairs.

These instruments of government - the individual, the class, the sect, the tribe, the parliament and the party struggling to achieve power have plundered the sovereignty of the masses and monopolized politics and authority for themselves.

THE GREEN BOOK guides the masses to an unprecedented practical system of direct democracy. No two intelligent people can dispute the fact that direct democracy is the ideal, but until now no practical method for its implementation has been devised. The Third Universal Theory, however, now provides us with a practical approach to direct democracy. The problem of democracy in the world will finally be solved. All that is left before the masses now is the struggle to eliminate all prevailing forms of dictatorial governments, be they parliament, sect, tribe, class, one-party system, two-party system or multi-party system, which falsely call themselves democracies.

True democracy has but one method and one theory. The dissimilarity and diversity of the systems claiming to be democratic do, in fact, provide evidence that they are not so. Authority of the people has but one face which can only be realized through Popular Conferences and People's Committees. There can be no democracy without Popular Conferences and Committees everywhere.

First, the people are divided into Basic Popular Conferences. Each Basic Popular Conference chooses its secretariat. The secretariats of all Popular Conferences together form Non-Basic Popular Conferences. Subsequently, the masses of the Basic Popular Conferences select administrative People's Committees to replace government administration. All public institutions are run by People's Committees which will be accountable to the Basic Popular Conferences which dictate the policy and supervise its execution. Thus, both the administration and the supervision become the people's and the outdated definition of democracy - democracy is the supervision of the government by the people - becomes obsolete. It will be replaced by the true definition: Democracy is the supervision of the people by the people.

All citizens who are members of these Popular Conferences belong, vocationally and functionally, to various sectors and have, therefore, to form themselves into their own professional Popular Conferences in addition to being, by virtue of citizenship, members of the Basic Popular Conferences or People's Committees. Subjects dealt with by the Popular Conferences and People's Committees will eventually take their final shape in the General People's Congress, which brings together the Secretariats of the Popular Conferences and People's Committees. Resolutions of the General People's Congress, which meets annually or periodically, are passed on to the Popular Conferences and People's Committees, which undertake the execution of those resolutions through the responsible committees, which are, in turn, accountable to the Basic Popular Conferences.

The General People's Congress is not a gathering of persons or members such as those of parliaments but, rather, a gathering of the Popular Conferences and People's Committees.

Thus, the problem of the instrument of government is naturally solved, and all dictatorial instruments disappear. The people become the instrument of government, and the dilemma of democracy in the world is conclusively solved.

7. THE LAW OF SOCIETY

Law represents the other problem, parallel to that of the instrument of government, which has not been resolved. Although it was dealt with in different periods of history, the problem still persists today.

For a committee or an assembly to be empowered to draft the law of society is both invalid and undemocratic. It is also invalid and undemocratic for the law of society to be abrogated or amended by individual, a committee, or an assembly.

What then is the law of society? Who drafts it and what is its relevance to democracy?

The natural law of any society is grounded in either tradition (custom) or religion. Any other attempt to draft law outside these two sources is invalid and illogical. Constitutions cannot be considered the law of society. A constitution is fundamentally a (man-made) positive law, and lacks the natural source from which it must derive its justification.

The problem of freedom in the modern age is that constitutions have become the law of societies. These constitutions are based solely on the premises of the instruments of dictatorial rule prevailing in the world today, ranging from the individual to the party. Proof of this are the differences existing in various constitutions, although human freedom is one and the same. The reason for the differences is the variation in the assumptions and values implicit in diverse instruments of government. This is how freedom becomes vulnerable under contemporary forms of government.

The method by which a specific modality of government seeks to dominate the people is contained in the constitution. The people are compelled to accept it by virtue of the laws derived from that constitution, which is itself the product of the tendencies within particular instruments of governments.

The laws of the dictatorial instruments of government have replaced the natural laws, i.e., positive law has replaced natural law. Consequently, ethical standards have become confused. The human being is essentially, physically and emotionally, the same everywhere. Because of this fact, natural laws are applicable to all. However, constitutions as conventional laws do not perceive human beings equally. This view has no justification, except for the fact that it reflects the will of the instrument of government, be it an individual, an assembly, a class or a party. That is why constitutions change when an alteration in the instruments of government takes place, indicating that a constitution is not natural law but reflects the drive of the instrument of government to serve its own purpose.

The abrogation of natural laws from human societies and their replacement by conventional laws is the fundamental danger that threatens freedom. Any ruling system must be made subservient to natural laws, not the reverse.

The fundamental law of society must not be subject to historical drafting or composition. Its importance lies in being the decisive criterion in light of which truth and falsehood, right and wrong, and individual rights and duties can be judged. Freedom is threatened unless society adheres to a sacred law with established rules that are not subject to alteration or change by any instrument of government. It is, rather, the responsibility of the instrument of government to adhere to the laws of society. Unfortunately, people the world over are currently ruled by manmade laws that can be changed or abrogated, depending upon the struggle for power among competing forms of government.

Conducting plebiscites on constitutions is often insufficient. Plebiscites are essentially a counterfeit of democracy since a "yes" or "no" is the only option. Moreover, under man-made law, people are compelled to vote on these plebiscites. Conducting a plebiscite on a constitution does not necessarily make the constitution the law of society. In other words, the status of a constitution will not be altered by a plebiscite; it will remain no more than the subject of a plebiscite.

The law of society is an eternal human heritage that does not belong only to the living. Therefore, drafting a constitution or conducting a plebiscite on it is a mockery.

The catalogues of man-made laws emanating from man-made constitutions are fraught with physical penalties directed against human beings, while tradition contains few such measures. Tradition lays down moral, non-physical penalties that conform to the intrinsic nature of humanity. Religion contains tradition and absorbs it; and tradition is a manifestation of the natural life of people. Its teachings comprise basic social guidelines and answers to the fundamental questions of existence.

Most physical penalties are deferred to a future judgment. This is the most appropriate law affording due respect to the human being. Religion does not provide for prompt penalties, save in certain compelling instances necessary to the well-being of society.

Religion contains tradition, and tradition is an expression of the natural life of the people. Therefore, religion is an affirmation of natural laws which are discerned therein. Laws which are not premised on religion and tradition are merely an invention by man to be used against his fellow man. Consequently, such laws are invalid because they do not emanate from the natural source of tradition and religion.

8. WHO SUPERVISES THE CONDUCT OF SOCIETY?

The question arises: who has the right to supervise society, and to point out deviations that may occur from the laws of society? Democratically, no one group can claim this right on behalf of society. Therefore, society alone supervises itself. It is dictatorial for any individual or group to claim the right of the supervision of the laws of the society, which is, democratically, the responsibility of the society as a whole. This can be arrived at through the democratic instrument of government that results from the organization of the society itself into Basic Popular Conferences, and through the government of these people through People's Committees and the General People's Congress - the national congress - where Secretariats of the Popular Conferences and the People's Committees convene. In accordance with this theory, the people become the instrument of government and, in turn, become their own supervisors. Society thus secures self-supervision over its laws.

9. HOW CAN SOCIETY REDIRECT ITS COURSE WHEN DEVIATIONS FROM ITS LAWS OCCUR?

If the instrument of government is dictatorial, as is the case in the world's political systems today, society's awareness of deviation from its laws is expressed only through violence to redirect its course, i.e., revolution against the instrument of government. Violence and revolution, even though they reflect the sentiments of society regarding deviation, do not constitute an exercise in which the whole of society takes part. Rather, violence and revolution are carried out by those who have the capability and courage to take the initiative and proclaim the will of society. However, this unilateral approach is dictatorial because the revolutionary initiative in itself provides the opportunity for a new instrument of government representing the people to arise. This means that the governing structure remains dictatorial. In addition, violence and effecting change by force are both undemocratic, even though they take place as a reaction against an undemocratic prior condition. The society that revolves around this concept is backward. What, then, is the solution?

The solution lies in the people being themselves the instrument of government whose authority is derived from Basic Popular Conferences and the General People's Congress; in eliminating government administration and replacing it by People's Committees; and finally, in the General People's Congress becoming a truly national convention where Basic Popular Conferences and People's Committees convene.

In such a system, if deviation takes place, it is then rectified by a total democratic revision, and not through the use of force. The process here is not a voluntary option for social change and treatment of social ills. It is, rather, an inevitable result of the nature of this democratic system because, in such a case, there is no outside group who can be held responsible for such deviation or against whom violence can be directed.

10. THE PRESS

An individual has the right to express himself or herself even if he or she behaves irrationally to demonstrate his or her insanity. Corporate bodies too have the right to express their corporate identity. The former represent only themselves and the latter represent those who share their corporate identity. Since society consists of private individuals and corporate bodies, the expression, for example, by an individual of his or her insanity does not mean that the other members of society are insane. Such expression reflects only in the individual's character. Likewise, corporate expression reflects only the interest or view of those making up the corporate body. For instance, a tobacco company, despite the fact that what it produces is harmful to health, expresses the interests of those who make up the company.

The press is a means of expression for society: it is not a means of expression for private individuals or corporate bodies. Therefore, logically and democratically, it should not belong to either one of them.

A newspaper owned by any individual is his or her own, and expresses only his or her point of view. Any claim that a newspaper represents public opinion is groundless because it actually expresses the viewpoint of that private individual. Democratically, private individuals should not be permitted to own any public means of publication or information. However, they have the right to express themselves by any means, even irrationally, to prove their insanity. Any journal issued by a professional sector, for example, is only a means of expression of that particular social group. It presents their own points of view and not that of the general public. This applies to all other corporate and private individuals in society.

The democratic press is that which is issued by a People's Committee, comprising all the groups of society. Only in this case, and not otherwise, will the press or any other information medium be democratic, expressing the viewpoints of the whole society, and representing all its groups.

If medical professionals issue a journal, it must be purely medical. Similarly, this applies to other groups. Private individuals have the right to express only their own, and not anyone else's opinions.

What is known as the problem of the freedom of the press in the world will be radically and democratically solved. Because it is by-product of the problem of democracy generally, the problem of freedom of the press cannot be solved independently of that of democracy in society as a whole. Therefore, the only solution to the persistent problem of democracy is through The Third Universal Theory.

According to this theory, the democratic system is a cohesive structure whose foundations are firmly laid on Basic Popular Conferences and People's Committees which convene in a General People's Congress. This is absolutely the only form of genuine democratic society.

In summary, the era of the masses, which follows the age of the republics, excites the feelings and dazzles the eyes. But even though the vision of this era denotes genuine freedom of the masses and their happy emancipation from the bonds of external authoritarian structures, it warns also of the dangers of a period of chaos and demagoguery, and the threat of a return to the authority of the individual, the sect and party, instead of the authority of the people.

Theoretically, this is genuine democracy but, realistically, the strong always rules, i.e., the stronger party in the society is the one that rules.

PART 2: THE ECONOMIC BASIS OF THE THIRD UNIVERSAL THEORY

11. THE ECONOMIC BASIS OF THE THIRD UNIVERSAL THEORY

Important historical developments contributing to the solution of the problem of work and wages - the relationship between producers and owners, workers and employers - have occurred in recent history. These developments include the determination of fixed working hours, overtime pay, leaves, minimal wages, profit sharing, the participation of workers in administration, the banning of arbitrary dismissal, social security, the right to strike, and other provisions contained in labour codes of almost all contemporary legislation. Of no less significance are changes in the realm of ownership, such as the enactment of laws transferring private ownership to the state, and also those limiting income. Despite these not inconsiderable developments in the history of economics, the problem still fundamentally exists, even though it has been made less severe than in past centuries through improvements, refinements and developments that have brought many benefits to the workers.

However, the economic problem still persists unsolved in the world. Attempts aimed at ownership have failed to solve the problems of producers. They are still wage-earners, despite the state ownership which may vary from the extreme right to the extreme left to the centre of the political spectrum.

Attempts to improve wages were equally significant to those that were aimed at the transferral of ownership. In the wake of the Industrial Revolution, benefits from wage negotiations secured for workers certain privileges that were guaranteed by legislation and protected by trade unions, thus improving the lot of the workers. As time passed, workers, technicians, and administrators have acquired certain rights which were previously unattainable. However, in reality, the economic problem still exists.

Attempts that were aimed at wages were contrived and reformative, and have failed to provide a solution. They were more of a charity than a recognition of the rights of the workers. Why do workers receive wages? Because they carry out a production process for the benefit of others who hire them to produce a certain product. In this case, they do not consume what they produce; rather, they are compelled to concede their product for wages. Hence, the sound rule: those who produce consume. Wage-earners, however improved their wages may be, are a type of slave.

Wage-earners are but slaves to the masters who hire them. They are temporary slaves, and their slavery lasts as long as they work for wages from employers, be they individuals or the state. The workers' relationship to the owner or the productive establishment, and to their own interests, is similar under all prevailing conditions in the world today, regardless of whether ownership is right or left. Even publicly-owned establishments give workers wages as well as other social benefits, similar to the charity endowed by the rich owners of economic establishments upon those who work for them.

Unlike the privately-owned establishment where income benefits the owner, the claim that the income from the public-owned establishment benefits all of the society, including the workers, is true only if we take into consideration the general welfare of the society and not the private well-being of the workers. Further, we would have to assume that the political authority controlling ownership is that of all the people, practised through the Popular Conferences and People's Committees, and not the authority of one class, one party, several parties, one sect, tribe, family, individual, or any form of representative authority. Failing this, what is received directly by the workers with respect to their own interests, in the form of wages, percentage of profits or social benefits, is the same as that received by workers in a private corporation. In both instances, the producers are wage-earners, despite the difference in ownership. Thus, this change in ownership has not solved the problem of the producer's right to benefit directly from what he produces, and not through the society nor through wages. The proof thereof is the fact that producers are still wage-earners despite the change in this state of ownership.

The ultimate solution lies in abolishing the wage-system, emancipating people from its bondage and reverting to the natural laws which defined relationships before the emergence of classes, forms of governments and man-made laws. These natural rules are the only measures that ought to govern human relations.

These natural rules have produced natural socialism based on equality among the components of economic production, and have maintained public consumption almost equal to natural production among individuals. The exploitation of man by man and the possession by some individuals of more of the general wealth than their needs required is a manifest departure from the natural rule and the beginning of distortion and corruption in the life of the human community. It heralds the start of the exploitative society.

If we analyse the factors of economic production from ancient times to the present, we always find that they essentially consist of certain basic production components, i.e., raw materials, means of production, and a producer. The natural rule of equality requires that each of these components receives a share of this production. Because production cannot be achieved without the essential role of each of these components, it has to be equally divided amongst them. The preponderance of one of them contravenes the natural rule of equality and becomes an encroachment upon the others' rights. Thus, each must be awarded an equal share, regardless of the number of components in the process of production. If the components are two, each receives half of the production; if three, then one-third.

Applying this natural rule to both ancient and modern situations, we arrive at the following. At the stage of manual production, the process of production resulted from raw material and a producer. Later, new means of production were added to the process. Animals, utilized as power units, constitute a good example. Gradually, machines replaced animals, types and amounts of raw materials evolved from the simple and inexpensive to the valuable and complex. Likewise, the unskilled workers became skilled workers and engineers; their former huge numbers dwindling to a few specialized technicians.

Despite the fact that components have qualitatively and quantitatively changed, their essential role in production has remained basically unaltered. For example, iron ore, a component of both past and present production, was manufactured primitively by iron smiths into knives, axes, spears, etc. The same iron ore is now manufactured by engineers and technicians by means of smelting furnaces into all kinds of machines, engines and vehicles. The animal - horse, mule, camel, or the like - which was a component of production, has been replaced by factories and huge machines. Production, based upon primitive tools, is now founded upon sophisticated technical instruments. Despite these tremendous changes, the components of natural production remain basically the same. This consistency inevitably necessitates returning to sound natural rules to solve the economic problems that are the result of all previous historical attempts to formulate solutions that ignore these rules.

All previous historical theories tackled the economic problem either from the angle of ownership of any of the components of production, or from that of wages for production. They failed to solve the real problem; the problem of production itself. Thus, the most important characteristic of economic order prevailing in the world today is a wage system that deprives the workers of any right to the products being produced, be it for the society or for a private establishment.

An industrial establishment is composed of material for production, machines and workers. Production is achieved by workers manufacturing materials and using machines. Thus, manufactured goods would not have been ready for use and consumption had they not gone through a production process requiring raw materials, factories, and workers. Clearly, without basic raw materials, the factory cannot operate and without the factory, raw materials will not be manufactured. Likewise, without producers, the factory comes to a halt. Thus, the three factors are equally essential to the process of production, and without them there can be no production. The absence of any one of these components cannot be replaced by the others. Therefore, the natural rule necessitates each component receiving an equal share of the benefits of production. It is not only the factory that is important, but those who consume its production as well.

The same is applicable to agricultural production processes resulting from only two components: man and land. The product must be divided equally into two shares congruent with the number of production components. Furthermore, if any additional mode, mechanical or otherwise is utilized in the process, production must be equally divided into three shares: the land, the farmer, and the means of production. Consequently, a socialist system emerges under which all production processes are governed by this natural rule.

The producers are the workers; they are called producers because the terms "worker," "labourer," and "toiler" have become invalid. The traditional definition is revised because workers are undergoing qualitative and quantitative changes. The working class is declining proportionately to the advancement of science and technology.

Tasks once performed by a number of workers are now being carried out by a single machine. Operating a machine requires fewer workers; this has brought about a quantitative change in the labour force, while the replacement of physical force by technical skill has resulted in a qualitative change in the labour force.

The labour force has become a component of the production process. As a result of technical advancement, multitudes of unskilled toilers have been transformed into limited numbers of technicians, engineers and scientists. Consequently, trade unions will subsequently disappear and be replaced by syndicates of engineers and technicians. Scientific advancement is an irreversible gain for humankind. Thanks to this process, illiteracy will be eliminated and unskilled workers will become a temporary phenomenon destined to gradual disappearance. However, even in this new environment, persons will always remain the basic component in the production process.

12. NEED

The freedom of a human being is lacking if his or her needs are controlled by others, for need may lead to the enslavement of one person by another. Furthermore, exploitation is caused by need. Need is an intrinsic problem and conflict is initiated by the control of one's needs by another.

13. HOUSING

Housing is an essential need for both the individual and the family and should not be owned by others. Living in another's house, whether paying rent or not, compromises freedom. Attempts made by various countries to solve the housing problem did not provide a definite solution because such attempts did not target the ultimate solution - the necessity that people own their dwellings - but rather offered the reduction, increase, or standardization of rent, whether it went to privately or publicly-owned enterprise. In a socialist society, no one, including society itself, has the right to control people's needs. No one has the right to acquire a house additional to his or her own dwelling and that of his or her heirs for the purpose of renting it because this additional house is, in fact, a need of someone else. Acquiring it for such a purpose is the beginning of controlling the needs of others, and "in need freedom is latent".

14. INCOME

Income is an imperative need for man. In a socialist society, it should not be in the form of wages from any source or charity from any one. In this society, there are no wage-earners, but only partners. One's income is a private matter and should either be managed privately to meet one's needs or be a share from a production process of which one is an essential component. It should not be a wage in return for production.

15. MEANS OF TRANSPORTATION

Transportation is also a necessity both to the individual and to the family. It should not be owned by others. In a socialist society, no person or authority has the right to own a means of transportation for the purpose of renting it, for this also means controlling the needs of others.

16. LAND

Land is the private property of none. Rather, everyone has the right to beneficially utilize it by working, farming or pasturing as long as he and his heirs live on it - to satisfy their needs, but without employing others with or without a wage. If lands were privately owned, only the living would have a share in it.

Land is permanent, while those who benefit from the land undergo, in the course of time, changes in profession, capabilities and existence.

The aspiration of the new socialist society is to create a society which is happy because it is free. This can only be achieved by satisfying, man's material and spiritual needs, and that, in turn, comes about through the liberation of these needs from the control of others. Satisfaction of these needs must be attained without exploiting or enslaving others; otherwise, the aspirations of the new socialist society are contradicted.

Thus, the citizen in this new society secures his material needs either through self-employment, or by being a partner in a collectively-owned establishment, or by rendering public service to society which, in return, provides for his material needs.

Economic activity in the new socialist society is a productive one aimed at the satisfaction of material needs. It is not an unproductive activity, nor one which seeks profit for surplus savings beyond the satisfaction of such needs. This, according to the new socialist basis, is unacceptable. The legitimate purpose for private economic activities is only to satisfy one's needs because the wealth of the world, as well as that of each individual society, is finite at each stage. No one has the right to undertake an economic activity whereby wealth exceeding the satisfaction of one's needs can be amassed. Such accumulations are, in fact, the deprived right of others. One only has the right to save from his own production and not by employing others, or to save at the expense of his or her own needs and not of others. If economic activity is allowed to extend beyond the satisfaction of needs, some will acquire more than required for their needs while others will be deprived. The savings which are in excess of one's needs are another person's share of the wealth of society. Allowing private economic activity to amass wealth beyond the satisfaction of one's needs and employing others to satisfy one's needs or beyond, or to secure savings, is the very essence of exploitation.

Work for wages, in addition to being enslavement as previously mentioned, is void of incentives because the producer is a wage-earner and not a partner. Self-employed persons are undoubtedly devoted to their work because from it they satisfy their material needs. Likewise, those who work in a collective establishment are also devoted to their work because they are partners in it and they satisfy their material needs from the production. Whoever works for a wage, on the other hand, has little incentive to work.

Work for wages has failed to solve the problem of motivation for increasing and developing production. Whether it is a service or goods production, work for wages is continuously deteriorating because it is performed by unmotivated wage-earners.

EXAMPLES OF WAGE-LABOUR: FOR THE SOCIETY, FOR PRIVATE

ENTERPRISE, AND SELF-EMPLOYMENT:

First example:

(a) A worker produces ten apples for society. The society gives him one apple for his production and it fully satisfies his needs.

(b) A worker produces ten apples for society. The society gives him one apple for his production which does not satisfy his needs.

Second example:

A worker produces ten apples for another person and gets wages less than the price of one apple.

Third example:

A worker produces ten apples for himself.

The conclusion:

In the first example (a), because the worker's wages are limited to one unit which satisfies his needs, he has no incentive to increase his production. Thus, all the labour force that works for society is psychologically apathetic.

(b) The worker has no incentive even to produce because he cannot satisfy his needs from the wages. However, he continues working without any incentives because generally, like all members, he is forced to acquiesce to the working conditions of the society.

In the second example, the worker works basically to get wages and not to produce. Since his wages cannot satisfy his needs, the choices are either to look for another master to get a better price for his work, or be forced, as a matter of survival, to remain where he is.

In the third example, the self-employed alone is the one who produces eagerly and voluntarily.

In a socialist society, there is no possibility for private production to exceed the satisfaction of one's needs because satisfaction of needs at the expense or by means of others is not permitted. Moreover, socialist establishments operate only for the satisfaction of the needs of society. Accordingly, the third example demonstrates the sound basis of its economic production.

However, in all instances, even the bad ones production is associated with survival. The proof thereof is that, even though in capitalist societies production accumulates and expands in the hands of only a few owners who do not work but exploit the efforts of others, the toilers are still forced to produce in order to survive. However, THE GREEN BOOK not only solves the problem of material production but also prescribes a comprehensive solution for the problems facing human societies so that individuals may be totally liberated, materially and spiritually, in order to attain their happiness.

Other examples:

If we assume that the wealth of a society is ten units and its inhabitants are ten persons, then the share of each member is one-tenth of the total one unit per person. If some members of this society get more than one unit each, then a certain number from the society get nothing. Their share of the wealth of their society has been acquired by others. Hence, the presence of rich and poor in an exploitative society. Let us also suppose that five members of that particular society each own two units. In such a case, half of the society is deprived of their rights to the wealth of their society, for what should be theirs has been acquired by others.

If an individual of that society needs only one of the units of the wealth of the society to satisfy his needs, then those who possess more than one unit are, in fact, seizing the rights of other members of the society. Because the one unit is all that is required to satisfy the needs of an individual, the additional units are acquired for the purpose of savings. This can only be achieved at the expense of the needs of others; the acquisition of others' share in this wealth. This is the reason behind the existence of those who hoard and do not spend; those who save beyond the satisfaction of their needs; and the existence of those who beg and are deprived of their right to the wealth of the society and do not find enough to consume. Such is an act of plunder and theft, yet according to the unjust and exploitative rules governing such a society, it is legitimate and overt.

Any surplus beyond the satisfaction of needs should ultimately belong to all members of society. Individuals, however, have a right to effect savings from the share allocated to their own needs since it is the amassing of wealth beyond the satisfaction of one's needs that is an encroachment upon public wealth.

The industrious and skilful in a society have no right, as a result of this advantage, to take from the shares of others. They can use their talents to satisfy their own needs and save from those needs. Like any other member of the society, the aged and the mentally and physically disabled should have their fair share of the wealth of the society.

The wealth of a society may be likened to a supply establishment or a store providing a certain number of people with daily rations satisfying their needs. Each person has a right to save from such provisions what he wants, i.e., to consume or save whatever portions of his share he decides, utilizing his talents and skill for such purposes. However, those who use their talents to acquire excessively from the "supply establishment" are undoubtedly thieves. Therefore, those using their skill to acquire wealth exceeding the satisfaction of their needs are, in fact, infringing upon the public right, namely, the wealth of society which is like the store in the said example.

Disparity in the wealth of individuals in the new socialist society is not tolerated, save for those rendering certain services to the society for which they are accorded an amount congruent with their services. Individual shares only differ relative to the amount of production or public service rendered in excess.

Hence, human experiences through history have produced a new experiment in a unique attempt to culminate the struggle of persons to complete their freedom, to achieve happiness through satisfying their needs, to ward off exploitation by others, to put an end to tyranny, and to find a method to distribute the wealth of the society equitably, without exploiting others or compromising their needs. It is the theory of the fulfilment of needs for the emancipation of humanity.

The new socialist society is but a dialectical outcome of the unjust relationships prevailing in the world today. The new socialist society will introduce the natural solution - privately-owned property to satisfy one's needs without exploitation, and collective property in which the producers are partners replacing private enterprise, which is based on the production of others without recognizing their right to a just share of the product.

Whoever possesses the house in which you dwell, the vehicle in which you ride or the income on which you live, possesses your freedom, or part of it. Freedom is indivisible. For people to be happy, they must be free, and to be free, they must possess the possibility of satisfying their own needs. Whoever possesses the means of fulfilling your needs controls or exploits you, and may enslave you despite any legislation to the contrary.

The material needs of people that are basic and personal start with food, housing, clothing and transport and must be regarded as private and sacred and their satisfaction should not depend on hire.

To satisfy these material needs through rent, gives the original owner the right to interfere in your personal life and to control your imperative needs, even if the original owner be the society in general. The original owner can usurp your freedom and take away your happiness. The interference of the original owner may include repossessing your clothes, even leaving you naked on the street. Likewise, the owner of your means of transportation may leave you stranded on the sidewalk, and the owner of your house may make you homeless.

People's imperative needs cannot be regulated by legal or administrative procedures. They must be fundamentally implanted into the society in accordance with natural rules.

The aim of the socialist society is the happiness of the human being, which cannot be attained except by the establishment of one's material, and spiritual freedom. The achievement of freedom depends on the private and sacred attainment of man's needs.

One's needs should not be under the domination of others and should not be subject to plunder by any source in society, otherwise one will live in insecurity. Deprivation of the means of fulfilment compromises freedom because, in attempting to satisfy basic needs, one would be subject to the interference of outside forces in one's basic interests.

The transformation of existing societies of wage-earners into those of partners is inevitable as a dialectical outcome of the contradictory economic theories prevailing in the world today. It is also a dialectical outcome of the unjust relationship based on the wage system. None of these issues have been resolved to date.

The antagonistic force of the trade unions in the capitalist world is capable of replacing capitalistic wage societies by a society of partnerships. The possibility of a socialist revolution starts by producers taking over their share of the production. Consequently, the aims of the producers' strikes will change from demanding increases in wages to controlling their share in production. Guided by THE GREEN BOOK , this will sooner or later take place. The final step is for the new socialist society to reach a stage in which profit and money disappear. Society will become fully productive; the material needs of society will be met. In this final stage, profit will disappear, as will the need for money.

The recognition of profit is an acknowledgment of exploitation, for profit has no limit. Attempts so far to limit profit by various means have been reformative, not radical, intending to prohibit exploitation of man by man. The final solution lies in eradicating profit, but because profit is the dynamic force behind the economic process, eliminating profit is not a matter of decree but, rather, an outcome of the evolving socialist process. This solution can be attained when the material satisfaction of the needs of society and its members is achieved. Work to increase profit will itself lead to its final eradication.

17. DOMESTIC SERVANTS

Domestic servants, paid or unpaid, are a type of slave. Indeed, they are the slaves of the modern age.

Since the new socialist society is based on partnership and not on a wage system, natural socialist rules do not apply to domestic servants because they render services rather than production. Services have no tangible material product and cannot be divided into shares according to the natural socialist rule.

Domestic servants have no alternative but to work for wages, or even be unpaid in the worst of situations. As wage-earners are a type of slave and their slavery exists as long as they work for wages, domestic servants, whose position is lower than that of wage-earners in economic establishments and corporations, have an even greater need to be emancipated from the society of wage-labour and the society of slaves.

Domestic servants is a phenomenon that comes next to slavery.

The Third Universal Theory heralds emancipation from the fetters of injustice, despotism, exploitation, and economic and political hegemony, for the purpose of establishing a society of all the people where all are free and share equally in authority, wealth and arms. Freedom will then triumph definitively and universally.

THE GREEN BOOK thus defines the path of liberation to masses of wage-earners and domestic servants in order that human beings may achieve freedom. The struggle to liberate domestic servants from their status of slavery and to transform them into partners, where their material production can be divided into its necessary basic components, is an inevitable process. Households should be serviced by their habitants. Essential household services should not be performed by domestic servants, paid or unpaid, but by employees who can be promoted in rendering their services and can enjoy social and material benefits as any other public employee would.

PART 3: THE SOCIAL BASIS OF THE THIRD INTERNATIONAL THEORY

18. THE SOCIAL BASIS OF THE THIRD UNIVERSAL THEORY

The social factor, the national factor, is the dynamic force of human history. The social bond, which binds together human communities from the family through the tribe to the nation, is the basis for the movement of history.

Heroes in history are, by definition, those who have sacrificed for causes. But what causes? They sacrificed for the sake of others, but which others? They are those with whom they maintain a relationship. Therefore, the relationship between an individual and a group is a social one that governs the people's dealings amongst themselves. Nationalism, then, is the base upon which one nation emerges. Social causes are therefore national, and the national relationship is a social one. The social relationship is derived from society, i.e., the relationship among members of one nation. The social relationship is, therefore, a national relationship and the national is a social relationship. Even if small in number, communities or groups form one nation regardless of the individual relationship amongst its members. What is meant here by a community is that which is permanent because of the common national ties that govern it.

Historic movements are mass movements, i.e., the movement of one group in its own interests differentiated from the interests of other communities. These differentiations indicate the social characteristics that bind a community together. Mass movements are independent movements to assert the identity of a group conquered or oppressed by another group.

The struggle for authority happens within the group itself down to the level of the family, as was explained in Part 1 of THE GREEN BOOK: The Political Axis of the Third Universal Theory. A group movement is a nation's movement for its own interests. By virtue of its national structure, each group has common social needs which must be collectively satisfied. These needs are in no way individualistic; they are collective needs, rights, demands, or objectives of a nation which are linked by a single ethos. That is why these movements are called national movements. Contemporary national liberation movements are themselves social movements; they will not come to an end before every group is liberated from the domination of another group. The world is now passing through one of the regular cycles of the movement of history, namely, the social struggle in support of nationalism.

In the world of man, this is as much a historical reality as it is a social reality. That means that the national struggle - the social struggle - is the basis of the movement of history. It is stronger than all other factors since it is in the nature of the human group; it is in the nature of the nation; it is the nature of life itself. Other animals, apart from man, live in groups. Indeed, just as the community is the basis for the survival of all groups within the animal kingdom, so nationalism is the basis for the survival of nations.

Nations whose nationalism is destroyed are subject to ruin. Minorities, which are one of the main political problems in the world, are the outcome. They are nations whose nationalism has been destroyed and which are thus torn apart. The social factor is, therefore, a factor of life - a factor of survival. It is the nation's innate momentum for survival.

Nationalism in the human world and group instinct in the animal kingdom are like gravity in the domain of material and celestial bodies. If the sun lost its gravity, its gasses would explode and its unity would no longer exist. Accordingly, unity is the basis for survival. The factor of unity in any group is a social factor; in man's case, nationalism. For this reason, human communities struggle for their own national unity, the basis for their survival.

The national factor, the social bond, works automatically to impel a nation towards survival, in the same way that the gravity of an object works to keep it as one mass surrounding its centre. The dissolution and dispersion of atoms in an atomic bomb are the result of the explosion of the nucleus, which is the focus of gravitation for the particles around it. When the factor of unity in those component systems is destroyed and gravity is lost, every atom is separately dispersed. This is the nature of matter. It is an established natural law. To disregard it or to go against it is damaging to life. Similarly, man's life is damaged when he begins to disregard nationalism - the social factor - for it is the gravity of the group, the secret of its survival. Only the religious factor is a rival to the social factor in influencing the unity of a group. The religious factor may divide the national group or unite groups with different nationalisms; however, the social factor will eventually triumph. This has been the case throughout the ages. Historically, each nation had a religion. This was harmonious. Eventually, however, differences arose which became a genuine cause of conflict and instability in the lives of people throughout the ages.

A sound rule is that each nation should have a religion. For it to be otherwise is abnormal. Such an abnormality creates an unsound situation which becomes a real cause for disputes within one national group. There is no other solution but to be harmonious with the natural rule, i.e., each nation has a single religion. When the social factor is compatible with the religious factor, harmony prevails and the life of communities becomes stable, strong, and develops soundly.

Marriage is a process that can positively or negatively influence the social factor. Though, on a natural basis of freedom, both man and woman are free to accept whom they want and reject whom they do not want, marriage within a group, by its very nature, strengthens its unity and brings about collective growth in conformity with the social factor.

19. THE FAMILY

To the individual, the family is more important than the state. Mankind acknowledges the individual as a human being, and the individual acknowledges the family, which is his cradle, his origin, and his social umbrella. According to the law of nature, the human race is the individual and the family, but not the state. The human race has neither relations nor anything else to do with the state, which is an artificial political, economic, and sometimes military, system. The family is like a plant, with branches, stems, leaves and blossoms. Cultivating nature into farms and gardens is an artificial process that has no relevance to the plant itself. The fact that certain political, economic or military factors tie a number of families into one state does not necessarily link this system or its organization with humanity.

Similarly, any situation, position or proceeding that results in the dispersion, decline or loss of the family is inhuman, unnatural and oppressive, analogous to any procedure, measure or action that destroys a plant and its branches and withers its leaves and blossoms.

Societies in which the existence and unity of the family become threatened due to any circumstance, are similar to fields whose plants experience uprooting, drought, fire, weathering or death. The blossoming garden or field is one whose plants grow, blossom and pollinate naturally. The same holds true of human societies. The flourishing society is that in which the individual grows naturally within the family and the family within society. The individual is linked to the larger family of humankind like a leaf is to a branch or a branch to a tree. They have no value or life if they are separated. The same holds true for individuals if they are separated from their families - the individual without a family has no value or social life. If human society reaches the stage where the individual lives without a family, it would then become a society of tramps, without roots, like artificial plants.

20. THE TRIBE

A tribe is a family which has grown as a result of procreation. It follows that a tribe is an enlarged family. Similarly, a nation is a tribe which has grown through procreation. The nation, then, is an enlarged tribe. The world is a nation which has been diversified into various nations. The world, then, is an enlarged nation. The relationship which binds the family also binds the tribe, the nation, and the world. However, it weakens with the increase in number. The essence of humanity is that of nation, the essence of nation is that of the tribe, and the essence of the tribe is that of family. The degree of warmth involved in the relationship decreases proportionately with the increase in size of the social unit. This is an indisputable social fact denied only by those who are ignorant of it.

The social bond, cohesiveness, unity, intimacy and love are stronger at the family level than at the tribal level, stronger at the tribal level than that of the nation, and stronger at the level of the nation than that of the world.

Advantages, privileges, values and ideals based on social bonds exist where those bonds are natural and undoubtedly strong. They are stronger at the family level than at the level of the tribe, stronger at the tribal level than that of the nation, and stronger at the nation's level than that of the world. Thus, these social bonds, benefits, advantages and ideals associated with them are lost wherever the family, the tribe, the nation or humankind vanish or are lost. It is, therefore, of great importance for human society to maintain the cohesiveness of the family, the tribe, the nation and the world in order to benefit from the advantages, privileges, values and ideals yielded by the solidarity, cohesiveness, unity, intimacy and love of family, tribe, nation and humanity.

In the social sense, the familial society is better than that of the tribe, the tribal society is better than that of the nation, and the society of the nation is better than world society with respect to fellowship, affection, solidarity and benefits.

21. THE MERITS OF THE TRIBE

Since the tribe is a large family, it provides its members with much the same material benefits and social advantages that the family provides for its members, for the tribe is a secondary family. What must be emphasized is that, in the context of the tribe, an individual might indulge himself in an uncouth manner, something which he would not do within the family. However, because of the smallness in size of the family, immediate supervision is not exercised, unlike the tribe whose members continually feel that they are under its supervision. In view of these considerations, the tribe forms a behaviour pattern for its members, developing into a social education which is better and more noble than any school education. The tribe is a social school where its members are raised to absorb the high ideals which develop into a behaviour pattern for life. These become automatically rooted as the human being grows, unlike classroom education with its curricula - formally dictated and gradually lost with the growth of the individual. This is so because it is formal and compulsory and because the individual is aware of the fact that it is dictated to him.

The tribe is a natural social "umbrella" for social security. By virtue of social tribal traditions, the tribe provides for its members collective protection in the form of fines, revenge and defence; namely, social protection. Blood is the prime factor in the formation of the tribe, but it is not the only one because affiliation is also a factor in the formation of the tribe. With the passage of time, the differences between the factors of blood and affiliation disappear, leaving the tribe as one social and physical unit, though it remains fundamentally a unit of blood in origin.

22. THE NATION

The nation is the individual's national political "umbrella"; it is wider than the social "umbrella" provided by the tribe to its members. Tribalism damages nationalism because tribal allegiance weakens national loyalty and flourishes at its expense. In the same way, loyalty to the family flourishes at the expense of tribal loyalty and weakens it. National loyalty is essential to the nation but, at the same time, it is a threat to humanity.

The nation in the world community is similar, to the family in the tribe. The more the families of a tribe feud and become fanatical, the more the tribe is threatened. The family is threatened when its individual members feud and pursue only their personal interests. Similarly, if the tribes of a nation quarrel and pursue only their own interests, then the nation is undermined. National fanaticism expressed in the use of force against weak nations, or national progress which is at the expense of other nations, is evil and harmful to humanity. However, strong individuals who have self-respect and are aware of their own individual responsibilities are important and useful to the family, just as a strong and respectable family, which is aware of its importance, is socially and materially beneficial to the tribe. Equally useful to the whole world is a progressive, productive and civilized nation. The national political structure is damaged when it descends to a lower social level, namely, the family and tribe, and attempts to act in their manner and to adopt their views.

The nation is an enlarged family which has passed through the period of the tribe and through the diversification of tribes that have branched out from one common source. It also includes those members who affiliated themselves with its destiny. The family, likewise, grows into a nation only after passing through the period of the tribe and its diversification, as well as through the process of affiliation which comes about as a result of interaction between various communities in a society. Inevitably, this is achieved over a long period of time. Although the passage of time creates new nations, it also helps to fragment old ones. Common origin and common destiny, through affiliation, are the two historic bases for any nation, though origin ranks first and affiliation second. A nation is not defined only by origin, even though origin is its basis and beginning. In addition to its origin, a nation is formed by human affiliations through the course of history which induce a group of people to live in one area of land, develop a common history, form one heritage, and face the same destiny. A nation, irrespective of blood bond, is formed through a sense of belonging and a shared destiny.

But why has the map of the earth witnessed great nations that have disappeared to give way to the rise of other nations? Is the reason only political, without any relationship to the social aspect of The Third Universal Theory? Or, is it social and so properly the concern of this part of THE GREEN BOOK?

Let us see. The family is indisputably a social structure rather than a political one. The same applies to the tribe because it is a family which has reproduced and enlarged itself to become many families. Equally true, the nation is a tribe after it has grown and its branches have multiplied and become tribes.

The nation is also a social structure whose bond is nationalism; the tribe is a social structure whose bond is tribalism; the family is a social structure whose bond is family ties; and global society is a social structure whose bond is humanity. These facts are self-evident. There is then the political structure of states which form the political map of the world. But why does the map of the world keep changing from one age to the next? The reason is that political structures may, or may not, be consistent with social structures. When political structure and social reality are congruent, as in the case of the nation-state, it lasts and does not change. If a change is forced by external colonialism or internal collapse, it reappears under the banner of national struggle, national revival or national unity. When a political structure embraces more than one nation, its map will be torn up by each nation, gaining independence under the banner of its respective nationhood. Thus, the maps of the empires which the world has witnessed have been torn up because they were composed of a number of nations. When every nation clings strongly to its national identity and seeks independence, political empires are torn up and their components revert to their social origins. This is evidently clear through the history of the world when reviewed through the ages.

But why were those empires made up of different nations? The answer is that the state is not a social structure like the family, the tribe and the nation, but, rather, a political entity created by several factors, the simplest and foremost of which is nationalism. The national state is the only political form which is consistent with the natural social structure. Its existence lasts, unless it becomes subject to the tyranny of another stronger nationalism or unless its political structure, as a state, is affected by its social structure in the form of tribes, clans and families. A political structure is corrupted if it becomes subservient to the sectarian social structure of the family, tribe, or sect and adopts its characteristics.

Religious, economic and military factors also contribute to form a state which differs from the basic, national state.

A common religion, as well as the requirements of economics or military conquests, may create a state which embraces several nations. Thus, in one age, the world witnesses a state or an empire which will disintegrate in another age. When the spirit of nationalism emerges stronger than religious loyalties, or conflict flares up between different nationalisms which were brought together, for example, by one religion, each nation becomes independent and recovers its social structure. That empire, then, disappears. The role of religion resurfaces when the religious spirit emerges stronger than the spirit of nationalism. Consequently, the various nationalisms are unified under the banner of religion until the national role appears once again, and so on.

All states which are composed of several nationalities for whatever reason - religion, economics, military power or man-made ideology will be destroyed by national conflict until each nation obtains its independence, because the social factor will inevitably triumph over the political factor.

Despite political circumstances which necessitate the establishment of a state, the basis for the life of individuals is the family, and extends to the tribe, the nation, and eventually to all humanity. The essential factor is the social factor. Nationalism is a permanent factor. Stress should be laid on social reality and family care in order to bring up an integrated well-educated human. Care should then be given to the tribe as a social "umbrella" and a natural social school which develops its members at the post-family stage. The nation then follows. The individual learns social values mainly from the family and the tribe which form a natural social structure created by no particular individual. Taking care of the family is in the interest of the individual just as the care of the tribe is in the interest of the family, the individual and the nation; it is part of the national identity. The social factor, the national factor, is the real constant dynamic force behind history.

To disregard the national bond of human communities and to establish a political system in contradiction to social reality establishes only a temporary structure which will be destroyed by the movement of the social factor of those groups, i.e., the national integrity and dynamism of each community.

These facts are innate in the life of humankind and are not intellectual conjectures. Every individual in the world should be aware of these realities and work accordingly so that his actions may be worthwhile. To avoid deviation, disorder and damage in the life of human groups which are the result of a lack of understanding and respect for these principles of human life, it is necessary to know these proven realities.

23. WOMAN

It is an undisputed fact that both man and woman are human beings. It follows, as a self-evident fact, that woman and man are equal as human beings. Discrimination against woman by man is a flagrant act of oppression without justification for woman eats and drinks as man eats and drinks; woman loves and hates as man loves and hates; woman thinks, learns and comprehends as man thinks, learns and comprehends. Woman, like man, needs shelter, clothing, and transportation; woman feels hunger and thirst as man feels hunger and thirst; woman lives and dies as man lives and dies.

But why are there men and women? Human society is composed neither of men alone nor of women alone. It is made up naturally of men and women. Why were not only men created? Why were not only women created? After all, what is the difference between men and women or man and woman? Why was it necessary to create men and women? There must be a natural necessity for the existence of man and woman, rather than man only or woman only. It follows that neither of them is exactly like the other, and the fact that a natural difference exists between men and women is proved by the created existence of men and women. This necessarily means that there is a role for each one of them corresponding to the difference between them. Accordingly, there must be different prevailing conditions for each one in order that they perform their naturally different roles. To comprehend these roles, we must understand the difference in the created nature of man and woman, that is, the natural difference between the two.

Women are females and men are males. According to gynaecologists, women menstruate every month or so, while men, being male, do not menstruate or suffer during the monthly period. A woman, being a female, is naturally subject to monthly bleeding. When a woman does not menstruate, she is pregnant. If she is pregnant, she becomes, due to pregnancy, less active for about a year, which means that all her natural activities are seriously reduced until she delivers her baby. When she delivers her baby or has a miscarriage, she suffers puerperium, a condition attendant on delivery or miscarriage. As man does not get pregnant, he is not liable to the conditions which women, being female, suffer. Afterwards a woman may breast-feed the baby she bore. Breast-feeding continues for about two years. Breastfeeding means that a woman is so inseparable from her baby that her activity is seriously reduced. She becomes directly responsible for another person whom she assists in his or her biological functions; without this assistance that person would die. The man, on the other hand, neither conceives nor breast-feeds. End of gynaecological statement!

All these innate characteristics form differences because of which men and women are not the same. These characteristics in themselves are the realities that define male and female, men and women; they assign to each of them a different role or function in life. This means that men cannot replace women in carrying out these functions. It is worthy of consideration that these biological functions are a heavy burden, causing women great effort and suffering. However, without these functions which women perform, human life would come to an end. It follows that it is a natural function which is neither voluntary nor compulsory. It is an essential function, without which human life would come to a complete halt.

Deliberate interventions against conception form an alternative to human life. In addition to that, there exists partial deliberate intervention against conception, as well as against breast-feeding. All these are links in a chain of actions in contradiction to natural life, which is tantamount to murder. For a woman to kill herself in order not to conceive, deliver and breast-feed is within the realm of deliberate, artificial interventions, in contradiction with the nature of life epitomized by marriage, conception, breast-feeding, and maternity. They differ only in degree.

To dispense with the natural role of woman in maternity - nurseries replacing mothers - is a start in dispensing with the human society and transforming it into a merely biological society with an artificial way of life. To separate children from their mothers and to cram them into nurseries is a process by which they are transformed into something very close to chicks, for nurseries are similar to poultry farms into which chicks are crammed after they are hatched. Nothing else would be as appropriate and suitable to the human being and his dignity as natural motherhood. Children should be raised by their mothers in a family where the true principles of motherhood, fatherhood and comradeship of brothers and sisters prevail, and not in an institution resembling a poultry farm. Even poultry, like the rest of the members of the animal kingdom, need motherhood as a natural phase. Therefore, breeding them on farms similar to nurseries is against their natural growth. Even their meat is artificial rather than natural. Meat from mechanized poultry farms is not tasty and may not be nourishing because the chicks are not naturally bred and are not raised in the protective shade of natural motherhood. The meat of wild birds is more tasty and nourishing because they are naturally fed. As for children who have neither family nor shelter, society is their guardian, and only for them, should society establish nurseries and related institutions. It is better for them to be taken care of by society rather than by individuals who are not their parents.

If a test were carried out to discover whether the natural propensity of the child is towards its mother or the nursery. the child would opt for the mother and not the nursery.

Since the natural tendency of a child is towards its mother, she is the natural and proper person to give the child the protection of nursing. Sending a child to a nurseryfinancial freedom in place of its mother is coercive and oppressive and against its free and natural tendencies.

Natural growth for all living things is free and healthy growth. To substitute a nursery for a mother is coercive action against free and sound growth. Children who are shipped off to a nursery are consigned compulsorily or by exploitation and simple-mindedness. They are driven to nurseries purely by materialistic, and not by social, considerations. If coercion and childish simple-mindedness were removed, they would certainly reject the nursery and cling to their mothers. The only justification for such an unnatural and inhuman process is the fact that the woman is in a position unsuitable to her nature, i.e., she is compelled to perform duties which are unsocial and anti-motherhood.

A woman, whose created nature has assigned to her a natural role different from that of man, must be in an appropriate position to perform her natural role.

Motherhood is the female's function, not the male's. Consequently, it is unnatural to separate children from their mothers. Any attempt to take children away from their mothers is cfinancial freedomoercion, oppression and dictatorship. The mother who abandons her maternity contradicts her natural role in life. She must be provided with her rights, and with conditions which are non-coercive, unoppressive and appropriate to her natural role. She can then fulfill her natural role under natural conditions. If the woman is forced to abandon her natural role regarding conception and maternity, she falls victim to coercion and tyranny. A woman who needs work that renders her unable to perform her natural function is not free and is compelled to work by need, and "in need, freedom is latent".

Among suitable and even essential conditions which enable women to perform their natural role, which differs from that of men, are those very conditions which are proper for a human being who is incapacitated and burdened with pregnancy. Bearing another human being in her womb lessens her physical ability. It is unjust to place such a woman, in this stage of maternity, into circumstances of physical work incompatible with her condition. For pregnant women to perform such physical work is tantamount to punishment for their betrayal of their maternal role; it is the tax they pay for entering the realm of men, which is naturally alien to their own.

The belief, even if it is held by a woman, that she carries out physical labour of her own accord, is not, in fact, true. She performs the physical work only because a harsh materialistic society has placed her (without her being directly aware of it) into coercive circumstances. She has no alternative but to submit to the conditions of that society, even though she may think that she works of her own accord. In fact, the alleged basis that "there is no difference in any way between men and women", deprives woman of her freedom.

The phrase "in any way" is a monstrous deception. This idea will destroy the appropriate and necessary conditions which constitute the privilege which women ought to enjoy apart from men in accordance with their distinctive nature, and upon which their natural role in life is based.

To demand equality between man and woman in carrying heavy weights while the woman is pregnant is unjust and cruel. To demand equality between them in fasting and hardship while she is breast-feeding is unjust and cruel. To demand equality between them in any dirty work which stains her beauty and detracts from her femininity is unjust and cruel. Education that leads to work unsuitable for her nature is unjust and cruel as well.

There is no difference between men and women in all that concerns humanity. None of them should marry the other against his or her will, or divorce without a just trial or mutual agreement. Neither should a woman remarry without such agreement or divorce;

nor a man without divorce or consent. The woman is the owner of the house because it is one of the suitable and necessary conditions for a woman who menstruates, conceives, and cares for her children. The female is the owner of the maternity shelter, which is the house. Even in the animal world, which differs in many ways from that of the humans, and where maternity is also a duty according to nature, it is coercive to deprive the female of her shelter and the offspring of their mother.

Woman is female. Being female means she has a biological nature that is different from that of the male. The female's biological nature, differing as it does from that of the males, has imparted to women characteristics different from those of men in form and in essence. A woman's anatomy is different from that of a man's just as the female differs in plants and animals. This is a natural and incontrovertible fact. In the animal and plant kingdoms, the male is naturally created strong and aggressive, while the female is created beautiful and gentle. These are natural and eternal characteristics innate to living creatures, whether they are called human beings, animals or plants.

In view of his different nature and in line with the laws of nature, the male has played the role of the strong and striving not by design, but simply because he is created that way. The female has played the role of the beautiful and the gentle involuntarily because she was created so. This natural rule is just, partly because it is natural, and partly because it is the basic rule for freedom. All living creatures are created free and any interference with that freedom is coercion. Not to adhere to these natural roles and to lack concern for their limits amounts to a wanton act of corruption against the values of life itself. Nature has been designed to be in harmony with the inevitability of life, from what is being to what will become. The living creature is a being who inevitably lives until it is dead. Existence between the beginning and the end of life is based on a natural law, without choice or compulsion. It is natural. It is natural freedom.

In the animal, plant and human realms, there must be a male and a female for life to occur from its beginning to its end. Not only do they exist but they have to exercise, with absolute efficiency, the natural role for which they have been created. If their role is not being efficiently performed, there must be some defect in the organization of life caused by historical circumstances. This is the case of societies almost everywhere in the world today as they confuse the roles of men and women and endeavour to transform women into men. In harmony with nature and its subsequent purpose, men and women must be creative within their respective roles. To resist is retrogressive; it is directed against nature and destroys the basis of freedom, for it is hostile to both life and survival. Men and women must perform, not abandon, the roles for which they are created.

Abandoning their role, or even a part of it, only occurs as a result of coercive conditions and under abnormal circumstances. The woman who rejects pregnancy, marriage, beautification and femininity for reasons of health abandons her natural role in life under these coercive conditions of ill health. The woman who rejects marriage, pregnancy or motherhood because of work abandons her natural role under similar coercive conditions. The woman who rejects marriage, pregnancy or maternity without any concrete cause abandons her natural role as a result of a coercive and morally deviant circumstances. Thus, abandoning the natural roles of female and male in life can only occur under unnatural conditions which are contrary to freedom and are a threat to survival. Consequently, there must be a world revolution which puts an end to all materialistic conditions hindering women from performing their natural role in life, and so drives them to carry out men's duties in order to attain equal rights. Such revolution will inevitably take place, particularly in industrial societies, as a response to the instinct of survival, even without any instigator of revolution such as THE GREEN BOOK.

All societies today look upon women as little more than commodities. The East regards her as a commodity to be bought and sold, while the West does not recognize her femininity.

Driving woman to do man's work is a flagrant aggression against the femininity with which she is naturally provided and which defines a natural purpose essential to life. Man's work obscures woman's beautiful features which are created for female roles. They are like blossoms which are created to attract pollen and to produce seeds. If we did away with the blossoms, the role of plants in life would come to an end. The natural embellishment in butterflies and birds and animal females exists to that natural vital purpose. If a woman carries out men's work, she risks being transformed into a man, abandoning her role and her beauty. A woman has full right to live without being forced to change into a man and to give up her femininity.

Physical structure, which is naturally different in men and women, leads to differences in the functions of the organs, which in turn leads to differences in the psyche, mood, emotions, as well as in physical appearance. A woman is tender; a woman is pretty; a woman weeps easily and is easily frightened. In general, women are gentle and men are aggressive by virtue of their inbred nature.

To ignore natural differences between men and women and to mix their roles is an absolutely uncivilized attitude, hostile to the laws of nature, destructive to human life, and a genuine cause for the wretchedness of human social life.

Modern industrial societies, which have made women adapt to the same physical work as men at the expense of their femininity and their natural role in terms of beauty, maternity and serenity, are materialistic and uncivilized. To imitate them is as stupid as it is dangerous to civilization and humanity.

The question, then, is not whether women should or should not work, for this is a ridiculous materialistic presentation of the case. Work should be provided by the society to all able members who need work - men and women on the condition that individuals work in their own fields and not be coerced into carrying out unsuitable work.

For children to find themselves under adult working conditions is unjust and dictatorial. It is equally unjust and dictatorial for women to find themselves under the working conditions of men.

Freedom means that every human being gets proper education which qualifies him or her for the work which suits him or her. Dictatorship means that human beings are taught that which is not suitable for them, and are forced to do unsuitable work. Work which is appropriate to men is not necessarily appropriate to women, and knowledge that is proper for children does not necessarily suit adults.

There is no difference in human rights between man and woman, the child and the adult, but there is no absolute identity between them as regards their duties.

24. MINORITIES

What is a minority? What are its rights and responsibilities? How can the problem of minorities be solved according to the solution to various human problems presented by The Third Universal Theory?

There are only two types of minorities. One of them belongs to a nation which provides it with a social framework, while the other has no nation and forms its own social framework. The latter is the one that forms one of the historic groups which eventually constitute a nation by virtue of a sense of belonging and a common destiny.

It is now clear that such a minority has its own social rights. Any encroachment on these rights by any majority is an act of injustice. Social characteristics are inherent and cannot be given or taken away. The political and economic problems of minorities can only be solved within a society controlled by the masses in whose hands power, wealth and arms should be placed. To view the minority as a political and economic substrata is dictatorial and unjust.

25. BLACK PEOPLE WILL PREVAIL IN THE WORLD

The latest age of slavery has been the enslavement of Blacks by White people. The memory of this age will persist in the thinking of Black people until they have vindicated themselves.

This tragic and historic event, the resulting bitter feeling, and the yearning or the vindication of a whole race, constitute a psychological motivation of Black people to vengeance and triumph that cannot be disregarded. In addition, the inevitable cycle of social history, which includes the Yellow people's domination of the world when it marched from Asia, and the White people's carrying out a wide-ranging colonialist movement covering all the continents of the world, is now giving way to the re-emergence of Black people.

Black people are now in a very backward social situation, but such backwardness works to bring about their numerical superiority because their low standard of living has shielded them from methods of birth control and family planning. Also, their old social traditions place no limit on marriages, leading to their accelerated growth. The population of other races has decreased because of birth control, restrictions on marriage, and constant occupation in work, unlike the Blacks, who tend to be less obsessive about work in a climate which is continuously hot.

26. EDUCATION

Education, or learning, is not necessarily that routinized curriculum and those classified subjects in textbooks which youths are forced to learn during specified hours while sitting in rows of desks. This type of education now prevailing all over the world is directed against human freedom. State-controlled education, which governments boast of whenever they are able to force it on their youths, is a method of suppressing freedom. It is a compulsory obliteration of a human being's talent, as well as a coercive directing of a human being's choices. It is an act of dictatorship destructive of freedom because it deprives people of their free choice, creativity and brilliance. To force a human being to learn according to a set curriculum is a dictatorial act. To impose certain subjects upon people is also a dictatorial act.

State-controlled and standardized education is, in fact, a forced stultification of the masses. All governments which set courses of education in terms of formal curricula and force people to learn those courses coerce their citizens. All methods of education prevailing in the world should be destroyed through a universal cultural revolution that frees the human mind from curricula of fanaticism which dictate a process of deliberate distortion of man's tastes, conceptual ability and mentality.

This does not mean that schools are to be closed and that people should turn their backs on education, as it may seem to superficial readers. On the contrary, it means. that society should provide all types of education, giving people the chance to choose freely any subjects they wish to learn. This requires a sufficient number of schools for all types of education. Insufficient numbers of schools restrict human freedom of choice, forcing them to learn only the subjects available, while depriving them of the natural right to choose because of the unavailability of other subjects. Societies which ban or monopolize knowledge are reactionary societies which are biased towards ignorance and are hostile to freedom. Societies which prohibit the teaching of religion are reactionary societies, biased towards ignorance and hostile to freedom. Societies which monopolize religious education are reactionary societies, biased towards ignorance and hostile to freedom. Equally so are the societies which distort the religions, civilizations and behaviour of others in the process of teaching those subjects. Societies which consider materialistic knowledge taboo are likewise reactionary societies, biased towards ignorance and hostile to freedom. Knowledge is a natural right of every human being of which no one has the right to deprive him or her under any pretext, except in a case where a person does something which deprives him or her of that right.

Ignorance will come to an end when everything is presented as it actually is and when knowledge about everything is available to each person in the manner that suits him or her.

27. MUSIC AND ART

Humans, being backward, are still unable to speak one common language. Until this human aspiration is attained, which seems impossible, the expression of joy and sorrow, of what is good and bad, beautiful and ugly, comfortable and miserable, mortal and eternal, love and hatred, the description of colours, sentiments, tastes and moods - all will be expressed according to the language each person speaks spontaneously. Behaviour itself will result from the reaction produced by the feeling that the language creates in the speaker's mind.

Learning a single language, whatever it may be, is not the solution for the time being. It is a problem that will inevitably remain without solution until the process of the unification of languages has passed through time, provided that the hereditary factor loses its effect on subsequent generations through the passage of sufficient time. The sentiment, taste and mood of ancestors form those of their descendants. If those ancestors spoke different languages and their children, on the contrary, speak a single language, the offspring would not necessarily share common tastes in virtue of speaking a common language. Such common tastes can be achieved only when the new language imparts the taste and the sense transmitted by inheritance from one generation to another.

If one group of people wears white clothes in mourning and another group puts on black, the sentiment of each group will be adjusted according to these two colours, i.e., one group rejects the black colour on such an occasion while the other one prefers it, and vice versa. Such a sentiment leaves its physical effect on the cells as well as on the genes in the body. This adaptation, will be transmitted by inheritance. The inheritors automatically reject the colour rejected by the legator as a result of inheriting the sentiment of their legator. Consequently, people are only harmonious with their own arts and heritage. They are not harmonious with the arts of others because of heredity, even though those people, who differ in heritage, speak a single common language.

Such a difference emerges between the groups of one people, even if it is on a small scale.

To learn a single language is not the problem, and to understand others' arts as a result of learning their language is also not the problem. The problem is the impossibility of a real intuitional adaptation to the language of others.

This will remain impossible until the effects of heredity, which are transmitted in the human body, come to an end.

Mankind is still backward because humans do not communicate in one inherited common language. It is only a matter of time before mankind, achieves that goal, unless civilization should relapse.

28. SPORT, HORSEMANSHlP AND THE STAGE

Sport is either private, like the prayer which one performs alone inside a closed room, or public, performed collectively in open places, like the prayer which is practised corporately in places of worship. The first type of sport concerns the individuals themselves, while the second type is of concern to all people. It must be practised by all and should not be left to anyone else to practise on their behalf. It is unreasonable for crowds to enter places of worship just to view a person or a group of people praying without taking part. It is equally unreasonable for crowds to enter playgrounds and arenas to watch a player of a team without participating themselves.

Sport is like praying, eating, and the feelings of coolness and warmth. It is unlikely that crowds will enter a restaurant just to look at a person or a group of people eat. It is also unlikely that they will let a person or a group or people enjoy warmth or ventilation on their behalf. It is equally illogical for the society to allow an individual or a team to monopolize sports while the society as a whole pays the costs of such a monopoly for the exclusive benefit of one person or team. In the same way, people should not allow an individual or a group, whether it is a party, class, sect, tribe or parliament, to replace them in deciding their destiny and in defining their needs.

Private sport is of concern only to those who practise it on their own and at their own expense. Public sport is a public need and the people cannot be either democratically or physically represented by others in its practice. Physically, the representative cannot transmit to others how his body and morale benefit from sport. Democratically, no individual or team has the right to monopolize sport, power, wealth or arms for themselves. Sporting clubs represent the basic organization of traditional sport in the world today. They retain all expenditure and public facilities allocated to sport in every state. These institutions are social monopolistic agencies like all dictatorial political instruments which monopolize authority, economic instruments which monopolize wealth, and traditional military instruments which monopolize arms. As the era of the masses does away with the instruments monopolizing power, wealth and arms, it will, inevitably, destroy the monopoly of social activity in such areas as sports, horsemanship, and so forth. The masses who queue to vote for a candidate to represent them in deciding their destiny act on the impossible assumption that this person will represent them and embody, on their behalf, their dignity, sovereignty and point of view. However, those masses who are robbed of their will and dignity are reduced to mere spectators, watching another person performing what they should naturally be doing themselves.

The same holds true of the crowds who, because of ignorance, fail to practise sport by and for themselves. They are fooled by monopolistic instruments which endeavour to stupefy them and divert them to indulging in laughter and applause instead. Sport, as a social activity, must be for the masses, just as power, wealth and arms should be in the hands of the people.

Public sport is for all the masses. It is right of all people for their health and recreational benefit. It is mere stupidity to leave its benefits to certain individuals and teams who monopolize these while the masses provide the facilities and pay the expenses for the establishment of public sports. The thousands who crowd stadiums to view, applaud and laugh are foolish people who have failed to carry out the activity themselves. They line up lethargically in the stands of the sports grounds, and applaud those heroes who wrest from them the initiative, dominate the field and control the sport and, in so doing, exploit the facilities that the masses provide. Originally, the public grandstands were designed to demarcate the masses from the playing fields and grounds; to prevent the masses from having access to the playing fields. When the masses march and play sport in the centre of playing fields and open spaces, stadiums will be vacant and become redundant. This will take place when the masses become aware of the fact; that sport is a public activity which must be practised rather than watched. This is more reasonable as an alternative than the present costum of a helpless apathetic majority that merely watches.

Grandstands will disappear because no one will be there to occupy them. Those who are unable to perform the roles of heroism in life, who are ignorant of the events of history; who fall short of envisaging the future, and who are not serious enough in their own lives, are the trivial people who fill the seats of the theatres and cinemas to watch the events of life in order to learn their course. They are like pupils who occupy school desks because they are uneducated and also initially illiterate.

Those who direct the course of life for themselves have no need to watch life working through actors on the stage or in the cinema. Horsemen who hold the reins of their horses likewise have no seat in the grandstands at the race course. If every person has a horse, no one will be there to watch and applaud. The sitting spectators are only those who are too helpless to perform this kind of activity because they are not horsemen.

Bedouin peoples show no interest in theatres and shows because they are very serious and industrious. As they have created a serious life, they ridicule acting. Bedouin societies also do not watch performers, but perform games and take part in joyful ceremonies because they naturally recognize the need for these activities and practise them spontaneously.

Boxing and wrestling are evidence that mankind has not rid itself of all savage behaviour. Inevitably it will come to an end when humanity ascends the ladder of civilization. Human sacrifice and pistol duels were familiar practices in previous stages of human evolution. However, those savage practices came to an end years ago. People now laugh at themselves and regret such acts. This will be the fate of boxing and wrestling after tens or hundreds of years. The more the people become civilized and sophisticated, the more they are able to ward off both the performance and the encouragement of these practices.

BONUS:

UNCLASSIFIED

HILLARY'S

EMAILS

EXPLAINING THE

REAL REASON

THEY MURDERED

MUAMMAR

GADDAFI

H: FRANCE'S CLIENT & Q'S GOLD. SID

From: Sidney Blumenthal

To: Hillary Clinton

Date: 2011-04-01 15:44

Subject: H: FRANCE'S CLIENT & Q'S GOLD. SID

UNCLASSIFIED U.S. Department of State

Case No. F-2014-20439 Doc No. C05779612

Date: 12/31/2015

RELEASE IN PART

B6

From: sbwhoeop

Sent: Saturday, April 2, 2011 10:44 PM

To:

Subject: H: France's client & Q's gold. Sid

Attachments: hrc memo France's client & Q's gold 040211.docx; hrc memo France's client & Q's gold

040211.docx

CONFIDENTIAL

April 2,.2011

For: Hillary

From: Sid

Re: France's client & Qaddafi's gold

1. A high ranking official on the National Libyan Council states that factions have developed within it. In part this reflects the cultivation by France in particular of clients among the rebels. General Abdelfateh Younis is the leading figure closest to the French, who are believed to have made payments of an unknown amount to him. Younis has told others on the NLC that the French have promised they will provide military trainers and arms. So far the men and materiel have not made an appearance. Instead, a few "risk assessment analysts" wielding clipboards have come and gone. Jabril, Jalil and others are impatient. It is understood that France

has clear economic interests at stake. Sarkozy's occasional emissary, the intellectual self-promoter Bernard Henri-Levy, is considered by those in the NLC who have dealt with him as a semi-useful, semi-joke figure.

2. Rumors swept the NLC upper. echelon this week that Qaddafi may be dead or maybe not.

3. Qaddafi has nearly bottomless financial resources to continue indefinitely, according to the latest report we have received: On April 2, 2011 sources with access to advisors to Salt al-Islam Qaddafi stated in strictest confidence that while the freezing of Libya's foreign bank accounts presents Muammar Qaddafi with serious challenges, his ability to equip and maintain his armed forces and intelligence services remains intact.

According to sensitive information available

to this these individuals, Qaddafi's government holds 143 tons of gold, and a similar amount in silver. During late March, 2011 these stocks were moved to SABHA (south west in the direction of the Libyan border with Niger and Chad); taken from the vaults of the Libyan Central Bank in Tripoli. This gold was accumulated prior to the current rebellion and was intended to be used to establish a pan-African currency based on the Libyan golden Dinar. This plan was designed to provide the Francophone African Countries with an alternative to the French.franc (CFA). (Source Comment: According to knowledgeable individuals this quantity of gold and silver is valued at more than $7 billion. French intelligence officers discovered this plan shortly after the current rebellion began, and this was one of the factors that influenced President Nicolas

Sarkozy's decision to commit France to the attack on Libya. According to these individuals Sarkozy's plans are driven by the following issues:

a. A desire to gain a greater share of Libya oil production,

b. Increase French influence in North Africa,

c. Improve his intemai political situation in France,

d. Provide the French military with an opportunity to reassert its position in the world,

e. Address the concern of his advisors over Qaddafi's long term plans to supplant France as the dominant power in Francophone Africa) On the afternoon of April 1, an individual with access to the National Libyan Council (NLC) stated in private that senior officials of the NLC believe that the rebel military forces are beginning to show signs of improved discipline and fighting spirit under some of the new military commanders, including Colonel Khalifha Haftar, the former commander of the anti- Qaddafi forces in the Libyan National Army (LNA). According to these sources, units defecting from Qaddafi's force are also taking a greater role in the fighting on behalf of the rebels:

SOURCES:

- https://wikileaks.org/clinton-emails/ emailid/6528

GREAT BOOKS/AUDIOBOOKS
THE GREEN BOOK BY MUAMMAR
GADDAFI
ON APPLE MUSIC, SPOTIFY, YOUTUBE,
YOUTUBE MUSIC
ARTIST: WORLDWIDE PROSPERITY

www.ingramcontent.com/pod-product-compliance
Lightning Source LLC
Chambersburg PA
CBHW032057020426
42335CB00011B/388